Plant Reproduction

Shelly C. Buchanan, M.S.

Consultant

Leann Iacuone, M.A.T., NBCT, ATC
Riverside Unified School District

Publishing Credits

Rachelle Cracchiolo, M.S.Ed., *Publisher*
Conni Medina, M.A.Ed., *Managing Editor*
Diana Kenney, M.A.Ed., NBCT, *Senior Editor*
Dona Herweck Rice, *Series Developer*
Robin Erickson, *Multimedia Designer*
Timothy Bradley, *Illustrator*

Image Credits: Cover, p.1 Shutterstock; p. 7 Andreas
S.Ween / Alamy; p.17 B.A.E. Inc. / Alamy; p.20 Bob Gibbons/
Science Source; p.19 David Nunuk/ Science Source; p.27
Getty Images/Gallo Images; pp.5, 6, 7,10, 11, 13, 14, 17, 19,
20, 21, 24, 25, 26, 31 iStock; pp.28,29 J. J. Rudisill; p.8, 22
John Serrao / Science Source; p.9 Krystyna Szulecka/FLPA
/ Science Source; p.12 Martin Shields / Science Source;
p.15 Merlin D. Tuttle; p.22 Nature Picture Library / Alamy;
pp.18, 32 Nigel Cattlin / Alamy; p.24 Nigel Cattlin / Science
Source; p.23 Scott Camazine/ Science Source; all other
images from Shutterstock.

Library of Congress Cataloging-in-Publication Data

Buchanan, Shelly, author.
 Plant reproduction / Shelly C. Buchanan, M.S.
   pages cm
 Summary: "Many plants catch your eye with their
amazing colors and shapes. But plants also reproduce in
amazing ways. From seeds to spores and pollination to
fertilization, plant reproduction is anything but ordinary"--
Provided by publisher.
 Audience: Grades 4-6.
 Includes index.
 ISBN 978-1-4807-4676-3 (pbk.) -- ISBN 1-4807-4676-2
(pbk.)
1. Plants--Reproduction--Juvenile literature. 2. Seeds--
Juvenile literature. 3. Pollination--Juvenile literature. I.
Title.
 QK825.B83 2016
 575.6--dc23
                                        2014045201

Teacher Created Materials

5301 Oceanus Drive
Huntington Beach, CA 92649-1030
http://www.tcmpub.com

ISBN 978-1-4807-4676-3

Table of Contents

Growing a New Generation

Every living thing, from a snail to a gorilla, is born and grows. And all living things eventually grow old and die. Some live for only a few days, like mayflies. Others live hundreds of years, like oak trees. Before they die, living things must reproduce or their species will die out. Just like any living thing, plants must also reproduce to survive.

There are over 400,000 kinds of plants in the world! But they all reproduce in two main ways. Some plants use seeds. Other plants reproduce using **spores**. Spores are plant cells that can make new plants. There are advantages and disadvantages to both types of reproduction. But there's no doubt that all living things benefit from having plants around. When it comes to life on Earth, the more plants, the better!

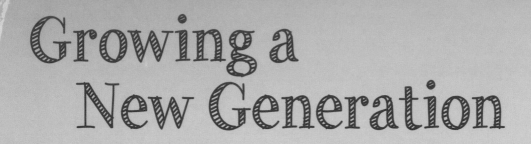

magnified spores under a fern leaf

More and More!

Seeds and spores are the most common ways for plants to reproduce. But there are other ways as well.

Budding
Sprouts of the original plant can be cut and then replanted to **clone** a new plant.

Fragmentation
Small parts of the plant or stem break off into the soil and grow into a new plant.

Propagation
Plants may produce horizontal stems that work their way into the ground, form roots, and grow a new plant.

Sowing Seeds

Many plants use seeds to produce their next generation. They may look plain, but seeds are amazing. A single seed holds all the instructions a plant needs to grow and survive. They may produce delicious apple trees or towering redwood trees. And it all fits in the palm of your hand!

Seeds are fertilized eggs. They contain a food supply and an **embryo**. Inside the embryo are the first leaves and roots of the new plant. A thick shell called a *seed coat* protects both the food and embryo. Sometimes, seeds wait a long time before growing. The conditions must be just right. Seeds might wait for warmer temperatures, or they might wait for more moisture. In the meantime, the food supply feeds the leaves and roots.

apricot seed

avocado seed

Coconut palms produce only a few large coconut seeds.

Trumpet trees
can produce
900,000 seeds!

angel's trumpet
seeds

Seeds, Seeds, Seeds

Different plants make different kinds of
seeds. Some produce just a few seeds.
Others create hundreds of thousands
of seeds. They want to increase their
chances of reproducing.

peas

vanilla seeds

pomegranate seeds

acorns

Gymnosperms

There are two types of plants that produce seeds: **gymnosperms** (JIM-nuh-spurms) and **angiosperms** (AN-jee-uh-spurms). Gymnosperms store their seeds in cones. Cones are the hard part of a plant that are exposed. Think of a pinecone. Most plants with cones are also called *conifers*. Most conifers are trees, such as firs, cypresses, pines, cedars, and redwoods. Some of these plants first appeared about 400 million years ago!

Conifers grow female and male cones. Male cones have small buds, or flowers, that come in a variety of colors, including red, purple, and yellow. Male cones make pollen. Pollen is the fine dust that helps to make new plants. When you think of cones, you probably think of large, plain cones. These are female cones. There are sticky scales that hold the eggs in place inside the female cones. Wind carries pollen from the male cone to the female cone. When pollen reaches the eggs, seeds are created. This process is called **fertilization**.

male jack pinecones

Once the seeds have developed, they're released from the cones. This often happens when cones drop to the ground. Wind may blow the seeds away. Or high temperatures may crack open the cones. Once the seeds are released, they need fertile ground to **germinate**. Then, the seeds can begin to grow into a plant.

8

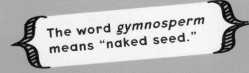

The word *gymnosperm* means "naked seed."

Conifers

- needle-shaped leaves with waxy coating
- cones grow at tips of branches
- pollinated by wind

conifer

Gnetophytes (NEE-toh-fahyts)

- shrub-like vines, trees
- large, leather-like leaves
- small cones grow off branches in clumps
- pollinated by insects

gnetophyte

Ginkgos

- fan-shaped leaves
- cones are small and dangle from branches
- pollinated by wind

Cycads (SAHY-kads)

- large, palm-like leaves
- large cones grow in the center of leaves
- seeds dispersed by animals

ginkgo

cycad

Angiosperms

The other type of plant that produces seeds is called an *angiosperm*. Most plants in the world are angiosperms. These plants make and protect their seeds inside flowers or fruit. Some plants only have flowers. Some have fruit and flowers. Both are angiosperms. When the seeds are released, they germinate in the ground. Then, they grow like gymnosperms. Plants have used this method of reproduction for over 135 million years.

One or the Other

Angiosperms live seasonally and die each year in the fall. They grow much quicker than gymnosperms and rely on animals to help them spread their seeds. There are two types of angiosperms: monocots and dicots.

Monocots

- one seed leaf
- petals in multiples of three
- leaf veins running in same direction

Angiosperms are sometimes called *flowering plants*. But their flowers aren't always easy to recognize. Some succulent plants, such as aloe and cactus, are angiosperms. Artichokes, brussels sprouts, cucumbers, and beans are angiosperms.

Flowers, fruits, and seeds are the reproductive parts of these types of plants. Many people eat these and enjoy their sweet taste. Look very closely the next time you eat strawberries—they're covered in tiny seeds. Birds, insects, and mammals all enjoy eating angiosperms.

Dicots
- two seed leaves
- stem or trunk grows in rings
- branched veins
- petals in multiples of five

Flower Power

Flowers are eye-catching. They come in many different colors, shapes, and sizes. Not only are they beautiful but they're also complex. Male and female parts work together to create seeds that will grow the next generation of plants.

anther

stigma

filament

stamen

petal

pistil

style

ovary

Pollination

The female part of a flower is called the *pistil*. It can usually be found in the very center of the flower. It includes the stigma, style, and ovary. The sticky stigma is at the top of the flower. Why do you think the stigma is covered in a sticky layer? Because it catches pollen. The style is the middle tube-like structure that connects the stigma to the ovary. That's where the egg is made.

The male part of a flower is called the *stamen*. This is where pollen is made. The stamen has two parts. The top part is the anther, which holds pollen. The bottom part is the filament. This acts like an arm and holds the anther to the flower. A flower is pollinated when pollen from the anther reaches the stigma.

Simply Perfect

Plants with flowers that have both male and female parts are called *perfect flowers*. Roses, lilies, and dandelions are all perfect flowers. Flowering plants with only male or only female parts are called *imperfect flowers*. Cucumber, pumpkin, and melon are all imperfect flowers.

cucumber

But how does the male's pollen get to the female's stigma? Similar to gymnosperms, wind blows the pollen. Rain can also help move pollen. But angiosperms have another advantage. Remember the brightly colored petals that surround these flowering plants? Well, they attract insects and other animals. These critters transport or move the pollen. Bees and hummingbirds are attracted to the sweet, pretty flowers. They pick up sticky pollen on their legs as they suck nectar from the plants. Then, they carry the pollen to the next flower. During this process, the pollen travels from the anther to the stigma.

Flowers know how to lure in **pollinators**. Bright white, pink, red, orange, and yellow colors flag down insects and birds. Some petals are marked with bright lines. Others have unique patterns. All these things make it possible for angiosperms to continue growing. And the most important moment happens when the pollen and the stigma meet. That's when **pollination** begins!

The honeysuckle flower tube is perfectly shaped for a hummingbird's beak.

The foxglove flower presents a cozy tunnel to help insects find nectar.

The bat-pollinated flower is pollinated by (you guessed it!) bats.

Not all plants display beautiful flowers. But they're still alive, so they must figure out a way to pollinate. These plants use wind for pollination. They don't need fancy petals to attract animals. They do, however, need to make a lot of pollen.

Have you ever noticed dust clouds blowing off plants? This is most common during the summer. Many grasses, shrubs, and trees create huge amounts of pollen. This pollen is tiny and light so the wind can carry it thousands of miles away from the parent plant.

Wind can be a tricky pollinator and not always reliable. Sometimes, there is a lot of wind. Other times, there isn't much wind at all. Also, wind isn't very precise. The pollen might not land on the stigma of the right plant. That's why these parent plants must make a huge amount of pollen. They need to increase their odds of reproducing.

plum

apricot

pluot

Offspring

A young plant created by two parent plants will be very similar to its parents. But it will also be a bit different. It will have a combination of traits from both parent plants. A pluot is a **hybrid** of a plum and an apricot.

Hay Fever Hassles

Pollen in the air can be a problem. The dusty bits easily pass into the nose, eyes, and mouth. Watery eyes, sneezing, and headaches are no fun! Yuck!

pollen under a microscope

Pine tree pollen blows away in the wind.

Fertilization

Pollination is just the first step in a flower's reproduction process. Once pollen reaches the stigma, it still must travel down the style. This happens naturally. The pollen needs to reach the ovary. The ovary is where the new plant will begin to form. Once the pollen makes its way to the ovary, it will find an egg. When the two combine, fertilization occurs. And a seed is born!

embryo

seed coat

food supply

Nutritious and Delicious

Seeds contain an embryo and its food supply. The food supply is full of nutritious things such as protein, amino acids, vitamins, and minerals. But these things aren't just good for plants! They're good for people, too.

butternut squash flowers

When the egg of the female squash flower is fertilized, a squash fruit begins to grow.

butternut squash

The word *ovary* comes from the Latin word for *egg*.

Eggs are stored in a plant's ovary. An egg has half the **genetic material** needed to form a new plant. These genes act like instructions, telling the plant how to grow and survive. Pollen has the other half of the genetic material. When an egg and pollen combine, a seed starts to form. It has all the instructions it needs to grow into an adult plant.

The process of fertilization takes just a few hours for some plants. For others, such as orchids, it takes much longer.

Spreading Seeds

Many seeds need to move away from their parent plant for survival. They need to find soil that can support their growth. A small area of land can only provide for a limited number of plants. The soil, sun, water and food supply in any single space are limited. The spreading of seeds increases the chance for seeds to take root and grow. This is called *seed dispersal*.

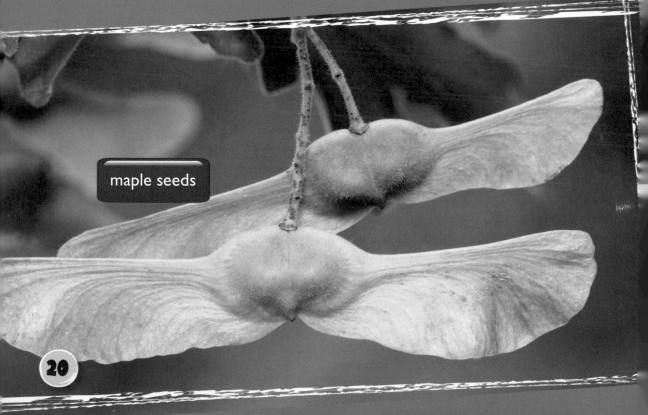

maple seeds

dandelion seed

coriander seeds

Simply Waiting

Some plants use gravity to disperse their seeds! Since the plant lives only one season, it simply lets its seeds fall to the ground. By the time the new plant has developed, the parent plant is gone.

The Millennium Seed Bank has collected and stored over 20,000 species of seeds in an effort to save endangered plants.

Seeds are dispersed in a variety of ways, depending on their size, shape, and texture. A huge coconut seed is unlikely to be seen flying through the air. And if it is, look out! But lightweight dandelion seeds are designed to travel by air. They float easily in the wind to new locations. They look like mini-helicopters! Seeds that travel by wind need to be small and light. Poppy and orchid seeds are very tiny. They shake right out of the fruit that produces them! Other seeds are designed to fly away with the slightest gust. Maple seeds have a propeller-like shape for flying.

Rainfall, streams, and rivers work as transportation systems for some seeds. Seeds that travel in water usually have a protective waterproof shell. Coconuts can travel by water for hundreds of miles. Many of these seeds have air bubbles that keep them afloat.

Animals also play a role in dispersing seeds. Birds might pick berries and carry them far away for a healthy lunchtime snack. The birds may spit out the seeds onto fresh new land. Sometimes, birds and other animals will eat the seeds. Many seeds contain a hard, protective coating that shelters the seed. Even when the seeds are digested, they move right through the animal and come out intact. The seeds are ready to grow in fertile ground.

black bear scat with seeds

Animal Dung Delivers

Seeds are an important part of many animals' diets. Some are digested, but many are not. The seeds that pass through animals are dispersed. Dung provides water, heat, and fertilizer for seeds. Thanks, animal friends!

People transport seeds, too! People carry seeds on their clothing. Some seeds have burs for catching rides on clothing or fur. Burs are the rough coating that covers the outside of a seed. You've probably gotten them stuck on your socks!

burdock burs

Carried Away

Nut trees drop their seeds to the ground, and squirrels, jays, and other animals can carry them away. They eat many of the seeds. But some they forget about. Those seeds grow into new plants far away from the parent tree.

Spreading Spores

Some plants don't have any seeds at all. So how do they reproduce? Mosses and ferns are some of the oldest plants living on Earth. For more than 300 million years, they have reproduced without using seeds.

A fern is a seedless plant. It reproduces with spores. First, it produces sporangia (spuh-RAN-jee-uh), which are structures that produce spores. Sporangia can be seen on the underside of the fern's fronds. They release spores into the wind. A spore is a cell that can make a new plant. Each spore stores the plant's genetic material. The spores grow into **gametophytes** (guh-MEE-tuh-fahyts). They make both female and male parts. When the female part is fertilized, it grows into a **sporophyte** (SPAWR-uh-fahyt). A mature sporophyte is a fern plant. And the cycle continues.

puffball fungus releasing spores

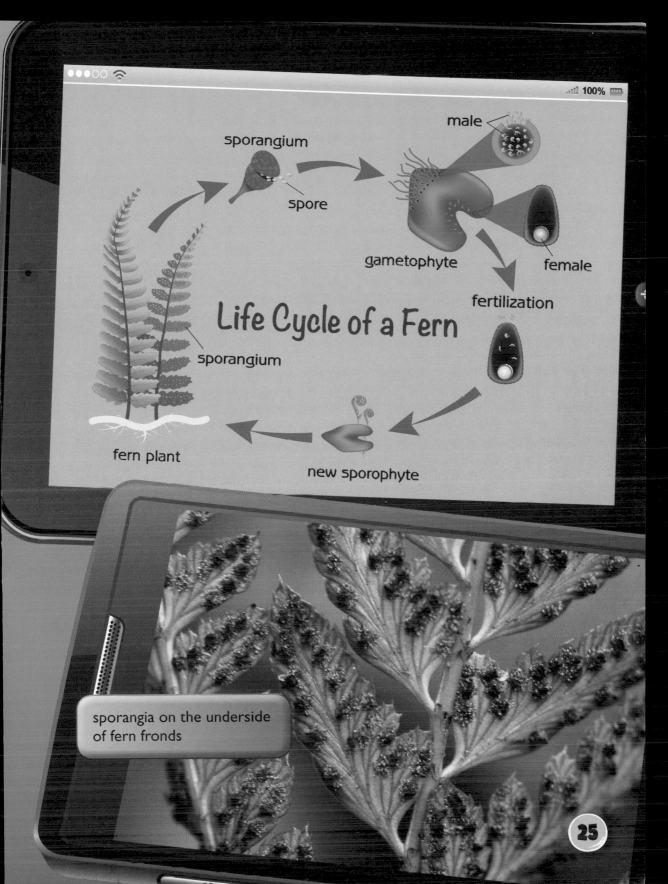

Life Cycle of a Fern

sporangium

spore

male

gametophyte

female

fertilization

fern plant

sporangium

new sporophyte

sporangia on the underside of fern fronds

Grow! Grow! Grow!

For over 400 million years, plants have reproduced successfully. The next time you're outside or in a garden, pay close attention to the types of plants that are around you. Are they gymnosperms with sturdy cones? Or are they angiosperms with lovely colorful flowers? Examine the seeds and think about the path they've traveled to get there. Those seeds help to make new plants. And without plants, there would be no us! We need plants to survive.

Like all living things, plants need to reproduce to survive. Wind, water, animals, and people all play a role in the process. So the next time you are enjoying refreshing lemonade or a warm apple pie, you can be thankful for plants. And with the knowledge you have, you can appreciate that slice of pie just a little bit more.

There's No Place Like Home

Even though plant seeds are spread far and wide, each one is best suited to a certain habitat. Over half of all plant species live in the rainforest. If their primary habitat is destroyed, these plants don't have a good chance of surviving.

Old, Old, Old

The oldest flowering plant in the world is a sacred fig named the *Jaya Sri Maha Bodhi* in Sri Lanka. It is 2,300 years old and is the oldest living tree planted by a human.

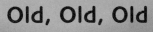

fig tree flower

Think Like a Scientist

Which plants have the most seeds? Experiment and find out!

What to Get

- 3 to 5 different fruits
- knife
- marker
- paper
- paper cups

What to Do

1 Choose three to five different fruits to examine. Create a chart similar to the one to the right. List the fruits you choose in the left column.

Fruit	Number of seeds

2 Write the name of a fruit on each cup.

3 Have an adult slice open each fruit. Dissect the fruits and separate the seeds. Put the seeds for each fruit in the matching cup.

4 Count the seeds for each piece of fruit. Record your findings on the chart. Analyze your data. Which fruits held the most seeds? Which fruits held the fewest? Why might each fruit hold different numbers of seeds?

Glossary

angiosperms—vascular plants in which seeds are enclosed in the ovary

clone—to make an exact copy of a person, an animal, or a plant

embryo—a living thing in the early stages of development

fertilization—combining male and female cells to produce a new living thing

gametophytes—plants in the life-cycle phase in which reproductive cells are produced

genetic material—information that controls characteristics of living things

germinate—to begin to grow and develop

gymnosperms—vascular plants that have seeds that are exposed

hybrid—an animal or plant that is produced from two animals or plants of different kinds

pollination—the transfer of pollen from one flower to another

pollinators—things that carry pollen from plant to plant

spores—cells made by some plants that are like a seed and can produce a new plant

sporophyte—a plant in the mature phase of its life cycle when spores are produced

Index

strawberry seed

Your Turn!

Focusing on Flowers

Find three different flowers. Ask an adult to cut each flower in half down the center. Identify and remove the parts of each flower. Can you name the parts that you see? How are the plant parts different for each flower? How are they similar? Tell your family and friends about what you discover.